Miracle on 34th Street, the Play

From the novel by
Valentine Davies

Based upon the Twentieth Century Fox motion
picture *Miracle on 34th Street*

Adapted by
MOUNTAIN COMMUNITY THEATER
of Ben Lomond, California
by
Peter Troxell, Rita Wadsworth,
Paul Sampson, Kathie Kratochvil, Ron Montana,
Phyllis Macy, Diana Troxell,
Lyle Troxell, Peter Gelblum
and
the many actors and crews who have
participated in the play

Dramatic Publishing
Woodstock, Illinois • Australia • New Zealand • South Africa

IMPORTANT BILLING AND CREDIT REQUIREMENTS

All producers of *Miracle on 34th Street, the Play* must give credit to Mountain Community Theater as the author of the play in all programs distributed in connection with performances of the play and in all instances in which the title of the play appears for purposes of advertising, publicizing or otherwise exploiting the play and/or a production. The name of Mountain Community Theater must also appear on a separate line, on which no other name appears, immediately following the title and must appear in size of type not less than fifty percent (50%) the size of the title type. *In all programs this notice must appear:*

"Produced by special arrangement with
THE DRAMATIC PUBLISHING COMPANY of Woodstock, Illinois"

In addition, all producers of the play must include the following acknowledgment on the title page of all programs distributed in connection with performances of the play and on all advertising and promotional materials:

"Based upon the Twentieth Century Fox motion picture
Miracle on 34th Street."

This credit must appear immediately following the name of Mountain Community Theater and must appear in size of type not less than fifty percent (50%) the size of the title type. Such billing need not be accorded on marquees and need not be accorded in ABC or teaser ads, radio or television ads or print ads of less than one-quarter (1/4) page if only the names of the title of the play, the name of the theater, and/or critics' quotes appear in such ads.

Comment

The story in this play is completely faithful to Valentine Davies' book, printed in 1947. The characters and their names are taken from the book. A few changes are as follows:

Either men or women may be cast in most of the roles, depending on actors available. Shellhammer, for instance, could be either a man or a woman. Only the roles of Kris Kringle, Doris Walker, Fred Gayley and Susan should remain as they originally were. Short scenes can be managed by using a small section of the stage, with limited lighting. Thus the set for the main scenes (e.g., Santa's dais in Macy's toy department or the courtroom) can remain undisturbed and darkened in the background.

A group of singers caroling during scene changes may provide an effective break that pleases audiences.

This play, like Valentine Davies' book and the Twentieth Century Fox motion picture, continues to be a delightful "twentieth century Christmas carol" (as it is called on the dust jacket of the book). We hope that groups presenting this play, and their audiences, will find the joy and spirit of Christmas so charmingly advocated here by the undaunted Kris Kringle.

Miracle on 34th Street, the Play was adapted from the 1947 novel by Valentine Davies by Mountain Community Theater, a non- profit, volunteer group of theater lovers, located in the town of Ben Lomond in the Santa Cruz Mountains of central California. The first production of *Miracle* occurred in November-December of 1982, the year that MCT was founded. Written by Peter Troxell and Rita Faye Wadsworth with Wadsworth directing, the play was highly successful and helped establish the group as a popular source of family entertainment in Santa Cruz County. The principal players in the first production were:

Kris Kringle . . . . Joseph Callaway
Doris Walker . . . . Kathie Kratochvil (Umstead)
Fred Gayley . . . . Paul Sampson
Susan Walker . . . . April Dawn McCaffery
Shellhammer . . . . Diana Wright Troxell
Sawyer . . . . Karen Solomon
Doctor Pierce . . . . Jerry Sheldon
Judge Harper . . . . Peter Troxell
Halloran . . . . Roy Wittrup
Finley . . . . John Cunningham
Mara . . . . Marilyn Painter
Macy . . . . Lencho Wehrmann
Gimble (Bloomingdale) . . . . Albert Kent
Mara Jr. . . . . Tabitha Altamirno
Al . . . . Andrew Schiller
Lou . . . . Randy Birch
Duncan . . . . David Jansen

Mountain Community Theater produced *Miracle* seven more times in 1983, 1984, 1987, 1992, 1994, 2002 and 2010, each time changing and adding action and dialogue to make the play more interesting. Writing for subsequent versions were: Paul Sampson, Kathie Kratochvil, Ron Montana, Phyllis Macy, Diana Troxell, Lyle Troxell and Peter Gelblum. It is the final 2010 version that is published here by Dramatic Publishing Company.

Miracle on 34th Street, the Play

A Play in Two Acts
For 3 men, 2 women, 1 girl, 14 men or women,
many extras including children

CAST OF CHARACTERS (in order of appearance)

DOCTOR PIERCE (m/w) . . . . physician at Maplewood Home
KRIS KRINGLE (m) . . . . Santa Claus
BAG LADY (w) . . . . at Thanksgiving Day parade
RICH PERSON (m/w) . . . . at Thanksgiving Day parade
SHELLHAMMER (m/w) . . . . Mrs. Walker's assistant
DORIS WALKER (w) . . . . personnel manager at Macy's
SUSAN WALKER (g) . . . . Doris' daughter, aged 7
FRED GAYLEY (m) . . . . a lawyer, neighbor and friend to
Doris and Susan
DRUNKEN SANTA (m) . . . . employee of Macy's
MACY (m/w) . . . owner and manager of Macy's Department Store
SAWYER (m/w) . . . . Macy's vocational guidance counselor
BLOOMINGDALE (m/w) . . . . owner and manager of
Bloomingdale's Department Store
JUDGE HARPER (m/w) . . . . of the New York State court
FINLEY (m/w) . . . . bailiff in Judge Harper's court
MARA (m/w) . . . . prosecuting attorney
HALLORAN (m/w) . . . Judge Harper's political campaign manager
DUNCAN (m/w) . . . . antelope keeper at the Central Park Zoo
MARA JR. (b/g) . . . . prosecuting attorney's child
AL & LOU (m/w) . . . . postal employees
TEENAGERS (3), CHILDREN (3), ELVES (4 to 8), PARENTS
(3)
PEDESTRIANS, SHOPPERS, POSTAL BAGGERS (3 or more
with doubling possible)

Note: Change names accordingly to fit male or female players.

7

ACT ONE

SCENE ONE

SCENE: *Central Park. The Friday after Thanksgiving.*

Carolers are singing, mingling with shoppers and parade participants. DOCTOR PIERCE and KRIS stroll in together amidst the bustle of the parade preparations. KRIS is carrying a suitcase.

PIERCE. Sure is a lovely day for the parade, Kris. I'm glad you suggested we come down and watch.

KRIS. Yes, it's a beautiful way to begin the season.

PIERCE. Do you want to sit down somewhere to watch this long parade?

KRIS. I don't mind standing. Or maybe I'll go sit on the curb with those children. *(Points.)*

BAG LADY *(to KRIS as she pulls a refundable bottle from a garbage can)*. Best place to watch from. It ain't a New York Christmas without Macy's parade, and the children love it.

KRIS. I saw a six-pack in the dumpster on 32nd Street. You might want to pick it up.

BAG LADY. Oh, thank you. I'll get it after the parade.

RICH PERSON *(to BAG LADY)*. My dear woman, why do you fish in garbage cans? It's repulsive!

BAG LADY. Because I find wonderful things in them. I can get money for this bottle. Every little bit helps. AND I'm doin' my Christmas shoppin'.

RICH PERSON. Christmas shopping!?

BAG LADY *(as she pulls out something of value, e.g., shoes)*. You'd be surprised to see what treasures people throw away.

RICH PERSON. Hrumph! I do my shopping in the privacy of my living room "The Home Shopping Club" on Channel 8. I just telephone my order and use my credit card. I can't be bothered plowing through all those crowds in the stores.

BAG LADY *(just as snooty as the RICH PERSON)*. You ought to be bothered a little. Besides, my shoppin' costs a lot less than yours! And it's appreciated just as much! It's the time and thought you put into it. That's how you show your love for your family—whatever way you do your shoppin'.

KRIS *(putting his arm around BAG LADY)*. I like your spirit. A real Christmas spirit is always a joy. *(BAG LADY smiles and leaves.)*

PIERCE. Well, you know that Christmas is always *big bucks* for the department stores. It's the season when they make up for the losses they have all year long.

KRIS. Christmas is more than big bucks, Doctor. Christmas is the one time that should be devoted to the pursuit of what we stubbornly avoid the rest of the year—peace, good will and helping others. What do you want for Christmas, Doctor?

PIERCE. I don't even think Santa Claus could get me what I want.

KRIS. Try me.

PIERCE *(hesitates)*. Hah. Well, if you say so. Maplewood's medical facility needs an X-ray machine. It could be helpful in so many situations. But it's *very* expensive.

KRIS. You shall have it, Doctor.

PIERCE. Kris, if I get that X-ray machine, I'll *know* you're Santa Claus.

KRIS. Just look in your stocking on Christmas morning.

PIERCE. Kris, we've never really discussed your having to leave Maplewood. I want you to know how sorry I am. I did everything I could, but the Board overruled me. They just won't allow us to keep anyone whom they have decided is mentally unsound.

KRIS. But I passed all those tests, didn't I?

PIERCE. I know you did. I've argued for you all along. But I just can't justify what they call paranoid thinking, even though you are not "harmful to yourself or others," to use the psychiatric jargon.

KRIS. You mean because I'm Santa Claus?

PIERCE. Because you *say* you're Santa Claus.

KRIS. But it happens to be true!

PIERCE. But the Board doesn't believe in Santa Claus. So… you're out.

KRIS *(considers a moment)*. What happens next?

PIERCE. Maplewood has an arrangement with the Mt. Hope Sanitarium.

KRIS. The "rubber room," huh?

PIERCE. For a public hospital, Mt. Hope is a comfortable and charming place… There's entertainment, TV, and… Kris, do you have any money?

KRIS. Sure. I've got $53.

PIERCE. That won't get you very far. You're not a young man anymore. It won't be easy for you to earn a living. If you can't support yourself, you'll become a ward of the state, and end up at Mt. Hope anyway. Why not avoid the disagreeable experience of living on the street?

KRIS. There's nothing wrong with me. I'll be *hanged* if I'll go to the funny farm!

PIERCE. What choice do you have?

KRIS. Wellll... The Central Park zookeeper is a friend of mine. Maybe I'll stay with him. The reindeer don't doubt my sanity.

PIERCE *(derogatory)*. Oh, Kris, please!

(The focus shifts to parade preparations.)

SHELLHAMMER. Well, Doris, after five years we have this parade business working pretty well, don't you think?

DORIS. Just as long as Mr. Macy is happy.

(SUSAN and FRED enter.)

SUSAN. I think the Barney float is better this year, Mother.

DORIS. Yes, Susan, we fixed his eyes so they roll, which makes him look more alive.

FRED. You watch your mother, Susan. You'll be able to handle this parade yourself by the time you're ten.

SHELLHAMMER. Would you believe eight?

(DRUNKEN SANTA CLAUS stumbles in, trips and falls.)

DRUNKEN SANTA CLAUS. Berry Dristmas! *(KRIS helps him up. DRUNKEN SANTA tries to crack his whip, but it flops.)*

KRIS. Allow me, sir. *(Cracks the whip smartly.)* You see, it's all in the wrist.

DRUNKEN SANTA CLAUS *(takes a swig from a bottle)*. Never works 'less you oil it zchuss a little. *(He chuckles at his joke.)*

KRIS. You should be ashamed of yourself! And in front of all these children. You're a disgrace to the uniform. Where's your Christmas spirit?

DRUNKEN SANTA CLAUS *(holding up bottle)*. Here! Right here… Gotta keep warm. *(He crosses his arms and slaps them. Drops bottle as he does so.)* Mmmmm warm.

SHELLHAMMER *(hasn't noticed what was happening)*. There's our Santa over there, Doris. *(As she looks in his direction, she realizes that he is drunk.)* Oh, my God! What do we do now?

DORIS *(following her gaze)*. How did we manage to get *him*?… Shelly, see if you can get him into the sleigh.

SHELLHAMMER. How?

DORIS. Get someone to help you shove, and tie him in, if you have to.

DRUNKEN SANTA CLAUS. I shink I'm going to be shleigh-shick. *(He passes out cold.)*

SUSAN *(staring at the prostrate SANTA)*. Mother, I don't think the people are going to like a Santa who's asleep.

DORIS. He's not his twinkling self, that's for sure.

(TWO CHILDREN are standing nearby looking on.)

CHILD NO. 1. Santa, please wake up.

SUSAN. That's not really Santa. He works for my mother at Macy's. If you want to see a Santa, they're ringing bells on every street corner in the city.

CHILD NO. 1. Those aren't real Santas.

CHILD NO. 2. We want to see Santa, himself!

SUSAN. I suppose you believe in the Easter bunny too?

PIERCE. This looks like a golden opportunity to solve both your problems, Kris. I think they need a replacement on the sleigh. You could spread the Christmas spirit and pay the rent at the same time.

KRIS. They haven't asked me.

PIERCE. *You* have to ask *them*. How can you sit and watch this? These children will be disappointed if there's no Santa.

KRIS. Doctor, you surprise me. Is that genuine Christmas spirit I hear, or are you pretending for my sake?

PIERCE. No, I've been thinking about what you said—giving and sharing. Whether you are the real Santa or not, you could certainly make those children believe you are.

KRIS. That's what it's all about, isn't it, Doctor? *(He stands and goes to DORIS.)* Excuse me. Is there anything I can do to help?

SHELLHAMMER *(seeing KRIS for the first time)*. I don't believe it! It's Santa Claus!

KRIS *(bowing slightly)*. My pleasure, ma'am.

DORIS *(taking him in)*. Shelly, it's a gift from—of course—from Santa Claus! *(To KRIS.)* Uh…sir, you can see what our problem is here. Would you fill in for us and play Santa in this parade?

KRIS. I'm not in the habit of substituting for intoxicated impostors. But, my dear, since the role fits me so perfectly… Which way to the dressing room?

DORIS. Shelly, get this gentleman suited up for the sleigh.

SHELLHAMMER. You bet! Right this way, sir. *(As she starts off the stage, she picks up DRUNKEN SANTA's bottle.)* And I'll get rid of this!

(Exit Shelly and KRIS; enter FRED who joins DORIS. ELVES and SUSAN are on stage during the following scene.)

FRED. Hello, Doris.

DORIS. Oh, hi, Fred. Susan's over talking to the elves. Could you get her and take her somewhere? There's so much going on right now that I don't have time to deal with the crazy ideas they'll put in her head.

FRED. Don't worry. I overheard the conversation. It was just about the North Pole.

DORIS. That's just what I mean! North Pole! North Pole! I appreciate your taking care of Susan, Mr. Gayley, and I'm very glad that you two get along so well. But we've been neighbors long enough for you to know that I have definite ideas about keeping her mind free of illusions. I've told you before that I *will not* have her believing in fairy tales, Mr. Gayley.

FRED *(teasing)*. Why not, Mrs. Walker?

DORIS *(relaxing)*. All right, Fred. Sorry to be so irritable. But I feel it's more important for her to understand reality. As a lawyer, I should think you would support that.

FRED. I didn't know you were raising a seven-year-old lawyer.

DORIS. It isn't a fairy-tale world we live in, Fred. She'll end up expecting that Prince Charming will come along, and he'll...and he'll... Well, Fred, you know that "happily ever after" just doesn't exist.

FRED. Are we talking about Susan, or about you? *(Pause.)* Look, I'm sorry, Doris. I'm sure your divorce was painful, but you can't stay bitter about it forever. Not all men will let a woman down and I don't think Susan's going to be any happier growing up to think so.

DORIS. I was devastated, Fred... Thank you for all your help, but please let me be Susan's parent.

SUSAN *(running to join DORIS and FRED)*. Hey, Mom, the elves are better this year. Their costumes actually fit.

FRED. Don't worry, Doris. Nobody will make up this kid's mind for her.

SCENE TWO

SCENE: *Macy's toy department, Santa's dais. The next morning.*

SHELLHAMMER *(to KRIS)*. Welcome aboard. I'm Ms. Shellhammer. It's my responsibility to train the new members of Macy's family of employees. Now, here's a list of the toys we want you to push, Mr. ahh...

KRIS. Kris Kringle.

SHELLHAMMER. Oh, really? That's very clever.

KRIS. The name's been in the family for generations.

SHELLHAMMER *(hastening past that one)*. Okay. Now we're overstocked on these toys. So if a child wants something we don't have, you should say, "Now, you might not like that. How would you like a *(contemporary toy should be inserted)*?" Understand?

KRIS. Why not give the children what they want?

SHELLHAMMER. Because it's Christmas. People will buy just about anything for the kids at Christmas. *You* can change kids' minds because they think you're really Santa Claus, see? So it's a good time to clear out our surplus inventory.

KRIS. Oh, the real economic spirit, huh?

SHELLHAMMER. Yes. And a Santa who helps move merchandise gets a little something extra in his Christmas stocking. Now, we mustn't keep the shoppers...uh...the children waiting. *(SHELLY exits. KRIS glares at the list, throws it in a trash receptacle, moves to the dais and sits, ready to start the day.)*

SCENE THREE

SCENE: *Same, the following Tuesday.*

Line of CHILDREN and PARENTS is waiting to talk to SANTA. ELVES escort CHILDREN to SANTA, give out candy canes. FRED and SUSAN are standing at rear. SUSAN watches closely.

KRIS. Hello, Sharon.

SHARON. How did you know my name?

KRIS. Because I'm Santa Claus. Now...what can I bring you for Christmas?

SHARON. I want a pink bike with ribbons on the handlebars.

KRIS. Well, you've been a good girl. I think that can be arranged.

SHARON'S PARENT *(sarcastic).* Thanks a lot, Santa. Do I look like I'm made of money? You should ask her if there's something else she'd like. Your store wants $125 for a bike like that. I've checked.

KRIS. Can you afford $55.95?

SHARON'S PARENT. Well... *(Looks puzzled.)* Ah...sure.

KRIS. Try Consumers Outlet on 30th Street.

SHARON'S PARENT *(stares at him).* I can't believe it! Macy's Santa Claus sending me to another store?

KRIS. It's not whether Consumers or Macy's sells the toy. The important thing is to make the child happy.

SHARON'S PARENT. This is wonderful. That's really good of you.

(Exits with SHARON. JOHNNY sits on SANTA's lap.)

KRIS. And what is your Christmas wish, young man?

JOHNNY. I want a fire engine—the kind that has real hoses and squirts real water, and I promise not to squirt it in the house.

KRIS. That's what you said about *(contemporary toy should be inserted)* last year!

JOHNNY. I know, but I really promise this time.

KRIS. All right, I'll accept your promise. But remember now.

JOHNNY'S PARENT. Why did you say that! I've been all over town and everybody's sold out.

KRIS. Bloomingdale's just got in a new shipment. They're on the fourth floor, second aisle on the left. And they're only $18.50—a marvelous bargain.

JOHNNY'S PARENT *(amazed)*. Bloomingdale's, huh? *(PARENT and JOHNNY leave, passing SHELLY.)*

SHELLHAMMER *(to JOHNNY'S PARENT)*. Thank you for shopping at Macy's.

JOHNNY'S PARENT. To tell the truth, I'm on my way to Bloomingdale's. Your Santa recommended it.

SHELLHAMMER. He *WHAT?!*

JOHNNY'S PARENT. And let me tell you…I think it's wonderful. That's the true Christmas spirit. He told me where I could get what my boy really wants. *(JOHNNY and PARENT exit.)*

SHELLHAMMER. Oohhh… What'll Mr. Macy say about *that?*

(DUTCH GIRL has been climbing onto SANTA's lap.)

DUTCH GIRL. *Sinterklaus!*

FOSTER MOTHER. This child has only recently arrived from an orphanage in Holland. She hasn't learned English yet. She wanted to see you so badly. She insists that "Sinterklaus" can speak Dutch. I hope you can pretend in some way.

DUTCH GIRL. *Sinterklaus!...Ik wil een pop en ik wil een bezoek van grootmoeder. Ik mis de mensen van net vaderland.*

g = h (e.g. *hrootmoeder*)
ee = a (as in late)
e = e (as in get)
ui = ou (as in out)
oe = o (as in vote)

FOSTER MOTHER. I'm sorry. I can't translate for you. I don't know Dutch well enough. I think she wants...

KRIS *(holds up his hand to silence FOSTER MOTHER)*. A doll and a visit with her grandmother in Holland. No problem. *(To DUTCH GIRL.)* Een pop en een bezoek van grootmoeder?

DUTCH GIRL *(giggles and laughs)*. Ja! Ja!

KRIS & DUTCH GIRL *(sing Christmas carol together—tune of* "Good King Wenceslas")*.

*Goede koning Wenceslaus keek uit op het feest van Stephen,
Als de sneeuw lag buiten, diep en vers en even.*

(DUTCH GIRL laughs, hugs SANTA, then leaves. MEGAN comes up next.)

KRIS. How are you today?

MEGAN. Mad.

KRIS. Tell me about it.

MEGAN. Me and my sister got into a fight. She told me the phone would grow onto my ear if I didn't get off of it.

KRIS. Kids like to tease each other, don't they? Remember the next time someone teases you, it's because that person is unhappy inside. You'll see, things will get better. Now, what do you want for Christmas.?

MEGAN. A telephone!

KRIS. Oh, I can see things will get better right away! *(Laughs.)*

(SUSAN and FRED are next in line. SUSAN has been listening intently to the previous interactions.)

FRED. Okay, Susan, it's your turn.

SUSAN. Do I have to?

FRED. Try it, anyway… For the sake of Macy's.

SUSAN *(as she approaches KRIS).* You know, of course, that this is ridiculous.

KRIS. And why don't you believe in Santa Claus, Susan?

SUSAN. How did you know that?

KRIS. I know lots of things. And what can Santa bring you for Christmas?

SUSAN. Nothing. Whatever I want my mother will get for me—provided it isn't too expensive. I know you're just a person my mother hired to play the part of Santa Claus. But I must admit, you're a little better than most. I can't even see the straps holding your beard on. It looks real. *(Pull on beard.)*

KRIS. That's because it *IS* real. And I'm real too.

(DORIS has entered another part of the stage, starts away on some business, suddenly spies SUSAN on KRIS's lap.)

SUSAN. Well, it was nice talking to you, anyway. But I don't think you ought to pretend to all these children that *you* are going to bring them what they want.

KRIS. Maybe they *will* get what they want this year, and so will you. *(SUSAN climbs off SANTA's lap, goes toward her mother.)*

FRED *(to KRIS)*. I'm sorry... She's a hard sell. Thanks for trying, anyway.

KRIS *(to FRED)*. My pleasure—and thank you for bringing her to me. I enjoy working on the tough cases.

FRED. It's really sad to see so much cynicism in a little girl like Susan.

KRIS. I agree. What she needs is an infusion of imagination. Maybe you and I can work on it together. *(KRIS exits. FRED follows after SUSAN, sees DORIS, who is glaring at him.)*

SUSAN. Mother, something funny happened. There was a Dutch girl in line who couldn't speak English, and the Santa spoke to her in Dutch. And they sang a song together.

DORIS. Susan, lots of people speak foreign languages. I speak French but that doesn't make me Joan of Arc! He's only a man I hired this morning, and even if there really were a Santa Claus, I doubt if he'd be working at Macy's. Now, I'd like you to sit right here *(indicates a seat)* while I speak to Fred a minute. Fred, would you please step this way? I just received Santa's employment record from the office. Perhaps you'd like to read it.

FRED *(takes card)*. Name: Kris Kringle. Age: As young as my tongue, and a little bit older than my teeth. Birthplace: North Pole. Next of kin: Donner, Dasher, Prancer, Dancer, Blitzen, Comet...

DORIS *(snatching card away from him)*. Does that convince you?... I think you'd better take Susan home now, if you don't mind. Apparently I have a job to do.

FRED. He still just seems like a nice old man...All right, I stand corrected... *(He returns to SUSAN.)* Come on, Susan, your mother has Christmas to manage.

(FRED and SUSAN exit as SHELLY approaches. In background KRIS prepares for break. ELVES bring out "Santa will return" sign, and begin to escort CHILDREN away.)

SHELLHAMMER. Doris, this new Santa is completely unacceptable. He refuses to push the backlog merchandise, and—you're not going to believe this—he's sending our customers to buy toys at other stores. *(DORIS reacts with incredulity.)* ...I'm not kidding... You've got to do something.

DORIS. What a coincidence. I was on my way to do just that. *(SHELLY exits. DORIS approaches KRIS who is now alone.)* Uh...Mr. Kringle. We've had a busy day, haven't we. Was it difficult for you?

KRIS. Getting accustomed to a new setting is always trying. But I have enjoyed the children.

DORIS. Maybe you've been trying a little too hard.

KRIS. What do you mean, Mrs. Walker?

DORIS. It seems you haven't been following Ms. Shellhammer's instructions.

KRIS. Oh, you mean to push the surplus toys? Yes, I decided not to do that.

DORIS. Oh, you did?

KRIS. I thought it was dishonest. Why should children have to pay for Macy's mistakes?

DORIS. That is not your decision to make, Mr. Kringle. And speaking of dishonesty, how do you explain this personnel card?

KRIS. It isn't dishonest.

DORIS. But, the things you put down on this form! We take our work seriously at Macy's, Mr. Kringle. We're not playing games. If you want a paycheck, you have to put proper information down on your personnel form.

KRIS. It all happens to be true. See...I verified it by signing at the bottom. *(Points.)*

DORIS. Then...you...really think you're Santa Claus?

KRIS *(firmly)*. Certainly not!

DORIS. Oh. Well, that's a relief.

KRIS. I *know* it for a fact!

DORIS *(stares at him)*. Well... You are welcome to whatever delusions you choose to live with...but...we cannot have a Santa who refers our customers to other stores. You can pick up your final check at the Personnel Department. I'm sorry it didn't work out.

KRIS. It strikes me as a bit ironic, Mrs. Walker, that you are firing Santa Claus for being Santa Claus! I was just making sure the children would get what they really want.

DORIS. Macy's is in business, Mr. Kringle, and we have to compete with other stores... Ooohhhh, I don't want to argue...I'll authorize a week's severance pay for you, Mr. Kringle. Now, Merry Christmas, and good-bye.

KRIS. Merry Christmas to you, Mrs. Walker. And don't worry. I won't hold this against you on Christmas Eve. *(Exits.)*

(MR. MACY and SHELLY approach DORIS.)

SHELLHAMMER. Uh...Doris...Mr. Macy would like to...

MACY. I'm perfectly capable of speaking for myself, Ms. Shellhammer.

DORIS. Is there a problem, Mr. Macy?

MACY. I will listen with great interest while you tell me who is responsible for our Santa sending customers to other stores. *(Pause. SHELLY stammers. DORIS winces.)*

DORIS. I take complete responsibility, Mr. Macy.

SHELLHAMMER. I instructed him to push our backlog stock, Mr. Macy, but he...

MACY. Well, then, *who* told him to send somebody to Bloomingdale's to get something we didn't have?

DORIS. Uh... We don't know, sir.

MACY. My office has been flooded with phone calls, faxes, letters...

DORIS. I'm really sorry, Mr. Macy, but I've taken care of it.

MACY. ...All messages of grateful appreciation from shoppers. This is the greatest goodwill advertising gimmick in years! It's positively revolutionary! I can see the headline: THE STORE WITH THE REAL CHRISTMAS SPIRIT! MACY'S SANTA RECOMMENDS BLOOMING-DALE'S! It's a breakthrough in advertising initiative, Mrs. Walker. The media will love it and Macy's will reap a harvest of publicity and goodwill.

DORIS *(dumbfounded)*. I'm so glad you're pleased.

MACY. This is the best Santa Claus we have ever had. *(As he starts away.)* And there'll be an extra bonus in both your Christmas stockings this year, ladies. *(Exits.)*

SHELLHAMMER. This must not be Tuesday after all. I'm still asleep and dreaming.

DORIS. It's Armageddon.

SHELLHAMMER. Huh?

DORIS. I just fired him.

SHELLHAMMER. You did *what?*

DORIS. You should see his personnel form. He's crazy. He really thinks he *is* Santa Claus.

SHELLHAMMER. Evidently so does Mr. Macy.

DORIS. I don't know what we'll do now.

SHELLHAMMER. Do you think Mr. Macy will fire us?

DORIS. Maybe it's not too late! *(She goes to nearest sales counter.)* Sylvia, have the operator page Kris Kringle, will you? *(SALESPERSON picks up phone. Page is heard in background during following interchange.)*

(Enter a few ELVES.)

ELF Z. Mrs. Walker, where is Santa? The line is stretching all the way to ladies' sportswear.

ELF Q. And we're almost out of candy canes!

SHELLHAMMER. She fired him.

ELF J. She fired Santa? In the middle of Christmas rush? What about the children?

ELF Q. Mrs. Walker. As the shop steward of Elves Local No. 10, I must lodge a formal grievance against management's capricious disrespect for the Christmas spirit.

DORIS. All right. We're trying to straighten the matter out right now.

ALL ELVES. Santa Claus goes, we walk!

DORIS. Oh, good grief! That's all I need. Striking elves!

(KRIS enters.)

KRIS. It wasn't necessary to page me, Mrs. Walker. I was going to bring the suit back to you.

SHELLHAMMER. Put it back on.

DORIS. Mr. Kringle, I owe you an apology. I'm afraid I was a bit hasty.

KRIS. Oh?

DORIS. I was mistaken about your policy of sending shoppers to other stores. As a matter of fact, Mr. Macy likes it.

KRIS. That's not reason enough, Mrs. Walker. Why should I come back just to increase Macy's profits? Pushing toys is not what Christmas is all about. We're so busy trying to make things go faster and look shinier so we can beat our competitor, that we're losing the spirit of giving from our heart. I see no reason why I should contribute to that kind of commercialism.

DORIS. You won't come back?

ELF Q. The union stands solidly behind you, Mr. Kringle.

DORIS *(to SHELLY)*. Here we are in the middle of the Christmas rush, and I lose the Santa who has worked a miracle, all because I didn't understand how miracles work. *(Pause. To KRIS.)* It really is more than a matter of profit, Mr. Kringle. Can't you see that Macy's needs you... *I* need you... And the children need you... Please? *(ELVES cheer.)*

SHELLHAMMER. Not to mention saving two wage slaves from being fired.

KRIS. Well...

DORIS. Would you stay if we promised not to ask you to push our overstock? Just be the Santa you want to be. Just be yourself.

KRIS. Now *that* I can do. *(ELVES cheer as they go toward the dais. ELVES help SANTA suit up again and start the line of CHILDREN. SANTA, CHILDREN and ELVES activity continues in background.)*

SHELLHAMMER. A masterful stroke, Mrs. Walker! *(She moves away.)*

(SAWYER approaches DORIS.)

SAWYER. You wanted to see me, Mrs. Walker?

DORIS. Oh, yes, Mr. Sawyer. *(She escorts him to another part of the stage.)* As our vocational guidance counselor, I hope you can help with a particular situation we have. *(They move out of earshot of clerks.)* We have a wonderful new Santa Claus in the Toy Department this year.

SAWYER. That's very admirable, Mrs. Walker.

DORIS. Not exactly. This man seems to be all right in every way—even a natural white beard. But he is actually convinced that he *is* Santa Claus.

SAWYER. Interesting.

DORIS. I was hoping you could help the old fellow a bit.

SAWYER. Hmmm… You mean he actually maintains his character outside of the work environment? *(DORIS nods.)* Oh, dear… Sounds to me like a classic case out of an abnormal psychology textbook. What other symptoms are there?

DORIS. None that I know of.

SAWYER. A persistent delusion. Very bad sign. Very… This sort of thing is usually deeply rooted in a failure to have emotional needs fulfilled in childhood. So the subject tries to personify the image of affection and gift giving. What is the subject's name?

DORIS. Kris Kringle.

SAWYER. You've got to be kidding!

DORIS. I wish that I were… But, please don't alarm him. He's a very valuable employee right now.

SAWYER. What do you want me to do?

DORIS. Just drop by and observe him, and then maybe arrange an interview. Keep it casual.

SAWYER. Leave it to me, Mrs. Walker. He'll never suspect…that I suspect. *(Exits.)*

(PIERCE approaches DORIS.)

PIERCE. Are you Doris Walker?

DORIS. Yes. May I help you?

PIERCE. Doctor Pierce. *(They shake hands.)* I'm the resident physician at the Maplewood Home, where Kris Kringle used to live.

DORIS. Oh, really? I think I'd like to talk to you.

PIERCE. I heard that you've hired Kris as Macy's Santa Claus. I'm so glad you gave him a chance.

DORIS. *Who* is he really, Doctor Pierce?

PIERCE. That's a good question. I've given it a lot of thought. He claims he's the real Kris Kringle, and if there really is a Santa Claus, he certainly fits the part.

DORIS *(appalled).* You don't honestly think he's Santa Claus, do you?

PIERCE. I didn't say that. I merely implied that from a purely philosophical point of view, he *could* be Santa Claus.

DORIS. Well, do you think he's Santa Claus?—philosophically speaking, of course.

PIERCE. It's one of those ideas that go round and round in your head— Like is snow, white? Or is red, red? Or when a tree falls in the forest, does it make a sound?

DORIS. Of course it does.

PIERCE. Does it? If you were standing there, it would, because the vibrations would bounce off your eardrums. But if there were no eardrums in the vicinity, could it still make a sound?

DORIS. I've heard that argument, but it could never be proven...

PIERCE. Or disproven. It's all in your perception. If nobody believed in Santa Claus, maybe he wouldn't exist. But millions of children all over the world do believe in Santa Claus. And Kris believes he is Santa Claus.

DORIS. He surely does.

PIERCE. We might say it's a case of "I think, therefore I am."

DORIS. You are still speaking philosophically, I assume.

PIERCE. When you live long enough, and deal with the world long enough, you find out that philosophically is really the only way to understand things. They make better sense that way.

DORIS. Unfortunately we have to be realistic in the retail business.

PIERCE. I understand... But I must tell you. Kris is perfectly harmless. There are thousands of people leading quite charming lives under similar delusions...

DORIS. I'm glad you said "delusions."

PIERCE. As I said, I've known Kris for years, and he's absolutely harmless. His delusion is a positive one. He just wants to bring happiness and the real spirit of Christmas to everyone. I just worry about him sometimes.

DORIS. Why?

PIERCE. Kris is an old man, and I'd hate to think of him wandering the streets of New York without a home to go to. If someone would just keep an eye on him...I mean after the store closes.

DORIS. You mean he has no place to live?

PIERCE. He can't stay at Maplewood anymore. They've discharged him.

DORIS. I'll see what I can do, Doctor Pierce. I appreciate your insights. I feel much more at ease after this conversation.

PIERCE. Thank *you*, Mrs. Walker. I know you won't regret having Kris on your staff. Have a Merry Christmas. *(Exits.)*

SCENE FOUR

SCENE: *Santa's dais, early the next morning.*

KRIS is alone on his "throne." SAWYER approaches.

SAWYER. Mr. Kringle, is it?

KRIS. Yes. That is one of the names I am called.

SAWYER. I'm Albert Sawyer, Macy's vocational guidance counselor.

KRIS. How do you do?

SAWYER. That remains to be seen. Uh…Mr. Kringle, before the customers start coming in, I'd like to get acquainted with you a little. As you are a new employee, store policy requires that I…uh…ask you some questions. Have you enjoyed your work here so far?

KRIS. I'd hardly call it work. To be honest with you, I normally do this sort of thing for free.

SAWYER. I see. So…uh…you normally promise gifts to children around Christmastime?

KRIS. I do my best.

SAWYER. How do you presume to provide all these gifts yourself?

KRIS. Santa Claus has a lot of influence in making things happen.

SAWYER. Uh-huh. And you sometimes go back to the North Pole at night to manufacture the gifts, right?

KRIS. Actually, no, I live with my reindeer.

SAWYER. Excuse me?

KRIS. Yes. I'm temporarily staying at the home of the zoo-keeper. I help him feed the reindeer and see that they are all right.

SAWYER. Oh… Well, let's move on. Can you tell me what three times five is, Mr. Kringle?

KRIS. Don't you know?

SAWYER. I want you to tell me.

KRIS. Fifteen, of course.

SAWYER. Good. Thank you. Now I want you to…

KRIS. Extend my arms and touch my nose, alternating between index fingers of each hand. *(Demonstrates.)* I also know this one: *(Touches thumb to each finger on his right hand.)* Do you know any new ones I haven't had before?

SAWYER. Who was the first president of the United States?

KRIS. George Washington. And do you know who was vice president under Grover Cleveland?

SAWYER. I have no idea. Mr. Kringle, I'm conducting this interview, if you don't mind. Now. Are you married?

KRIS. Is that a proposal?

SAWYER *(getting irritated)*. How many fingers am I holding up?

KRIS. Three. *(Leans close.)* My, my. I see that you bite your nails. Do these interviews make you nervous?

SAWYER. That's none of your business! Now, how much is three times five?

KRIS. Fifteen. The same as it was the first time you asked. Do you know that unconscious repetition is often a sign of overwork and stress? Are you getting enough rest, Mr. Sawyer?

SAWYER *(has reached his limit)*. That'll be all, Mr. Kringle!

KRIS. You could really use a nice vacation. Why don't you take a couple of weeks. I could talk to Mr. Macy for you.

(As SAWYER exits, he meets DORIS in another part of stage. ELVES start bringing CHILDREN in. Santa Claus activity continues in background.)

SAWYER. That...that...man! He definitely has a rampant psychosis!

DORIS. Who?

SAWYER. That Santa. That...Kris Kringle.

DORIS. Oh, come on, Sawyer. His doctor was here, and he assured me that Kris was perfectly harmless.

SAWYER. Perfectly harmless!... Cases like this often become violent when their delusions are attacked. If that man is allowed to continue to work here, I will take *no* responsibility for the consequences!

DORIS. That's all right. *I'll* take the responsibility, Mr. Sawyer. Don't worry about it.

SAWYER. If I'm the psychologist around here, I think my opinion should be respected... I warn you, Mrs. Walker, that if that man becomes violent and something happens... well, I'll be the first to say "I told you so."

(SAWYER storms off, bumping into SHELLY, as she approaches DORIS.)

SHELLHAMMER. Good heavens! What was that all about?

DORIS. Sawyer did a psychological evaluation of our Santa and apparently didn't get anywhere. His opinion is that Kris could become violent.

SHELLHAMMER. That would be a disaster!

DORIS. But I also had an interview with Doctor Pierce from the Maplewood Home where Kris has been living. He says Kris is just a sweet old man who thinks he's Santa Claus, and he wouldn't hurt anybody.

SHELLHAMMER. Do you believe the doctor?

DORIS. He said he has known Kris for a long time. Sawyer only talked to him for ten minutes.

SHELLHAMMER. Why did the doctor seek you out?

DORIS. He seems very fond of Kris and is rather protective of him. He's glad Kris has a job as Santa Claus, but he's worried about the hours after the store closes. He wants me to look out for him.

SHELLHAMMER. I think that's a splendid idea. And you're just the person to do it.

DORIS. What are you suggesting?… Not have him stay with me!… No way! I have enough responsibility with Susan, and at night I need to unwind.

SHELLHAMMER. Well… Maybe I can help out. We have a spare room. Kris can stay with us.

DORIS. You're a jewel, Shelly. I was hoping I could count on you.

SHELLHAMMER. Not so fast, Mrs. Walker… I'll have to talk it over with my husband first. It's his home too… I'll tell you what. You have Kris over for dinner tonight, and that'll give me time to talk to Arthur. I'll try to convince him that as a part of our Christmas spirit, we should have this nice old man as a *temporary* houseguest… I don't think I'll mention that he believes he's Santa Claus.

DORIS. What'll Arthur think when he's introduced to "Kris Kringle"?

SHELLHAMMER. Ohhh… I'll have to think of a way around that one.

DORIS. Okay. I appreciate it, Shelly. I'll talk to you later.

SCENE FIVE

SCENE: *Living room in Doris' apartment. That evening.*

DORIS, KRIS and SUSAN are sitting. Glasses of milk and plate of cookies are on coffee table.

KRIS. I enjoyed our dinner very much. Thank you for inviting me. I thought the milk and cookies for dessert was an especially nice touch. And I liked spending the evening with you and Susan.

SUSAN *(obviously delighted with the guest)*. Mr. Kringle, could you speak to me in that language you spoke in the store the other day?

DORIS. Susan, I think Mr. Kringle is tired.

KRIS. Not at all. I'd love to talk to her. Susan, come here.

DORIS. Excuse me. I've got to call Ms. Shellhammer. *(She exits to another room.)*

KRIS. Do you have a lot of friends in the building, Susan?

SUSAN. Yes, but I don't see them very much. The games they play are so childish. Today they were being animals. They asked me what kind of animal I wanted to be, but I didn't want to be an animal. It's so dumb.

KRIS. Why didn't you tell them you were a lion or a bear?

SUSAN. Because I'm not a lion. I'm a girl!

KRIS. But the other children weren't animals, either. They were just pretending.

SUSAN. That's what makes the game so silly.

KRIS. Do you know what imagination is, Susan?

SUSAN. That's when you see things that aren't really there.

KRIS. Yes, but it's more than that. Imagination is a place you can go to. A very wonderful country. You've heard of nations like England and Russia and Japan? *(SUSAN nods.)*

Well, imagi-Nation is a place like that. And the wonderful thing about that country is, once you get there, you can do anything you want.

SUSAN. Not *any*thing…

KRIS. For instance. How would you like to fly to Mars and be back by dinner time?

SUSAN. Oh, *that* wouldn't be possible.

KRIS. Or be the Statue of Liberty in the morning and fly south with a flock of geese in the afternoon? *(SUSAN smiles and nods in spite of herself.)* It's very simple. Want to give it a try?

SUSAN. Well, I guess I could try.

KRIS. Okay. Let's start with something easy. How would you like to be a bird flying in the sky?

SUSAN. I wouldn't know how to do that, Mr. Kringle.

KRIS. Sure you would! Now, stand up. Spread your arms out. That's right. And wave them up and down like wings… Fine. Now tilt sideways and turn. Keep on flapping your wings. That's it! Now you are *soaring* like a bird!

SUSAN *(running to him when the experiment is finished)*. I did it, Mr. Kringle. That was fun!

KRIS *(pause)*. Now tell me, if you were to believe that I was really Santa Claus, what would you ask me to bring you for Christmas?

SUSAN. Can you bring *big* presents?

KRIS. Since we are in the land of imagination, it could be any size.

SUSAN. I want a real house for Mother and me…and a real father to live in it with us.

KRIS *(jolted)*. You're right. That *is* a tall order, indeed.

SUSAN. Well, if you're really Santa, you can do it. And if you can't, then you're just a nice man with a white beard like Mother said.

KRIS. Susan, not everyone always gets her wish. That doesn't mean there isn't a Santa Claus. Some children wish for things they can never use—like a real locomotive, for example. And little girls sometimes wish for baby brothers or sisters, even though their parents wouldn't be able to care for them properly... Sometimes a person has to learn something, like how to love or how to behave better before Santa can grant the wish.

SUSAN. But I've wished for a father and a house for such a long time, Mr. Kringle.

KRIS. And the more you have wished for it, the more it will mean to you when it comes. If everyone got what he or she wanted right away, life wouldn't be half as much fun. So you see, Susan, there are a lot of reasons why a child's wish can't always come true.

SUSAN. A father and a house are really all I want—not toys.

(FRED knocks, enters.)

FRED. Hi there, Susan. How's my favorite girl? *(SUSAN runs to hug him. To KRIS.)* I'm Fred Gayley. I live in the next apartment.

KRIS. It's a pleasure to meet you, Mr. Gayley. I'm Kris Kringle.

FRED. Yes, I know.

(DORIS enters.)

DORIS. Susan, it's time for bed... Oh, hi, Fred. Have you two met?

KRIS. Yes, we just introduced ourselves.

DORIS. Mr. Kringle. I've found you a place to stay tonight. *(KRIS nods. Phone is heard ringing.)* Oh, there's my phone. Please wait a minute. *(She exits.)*

FRED *(to KRIS)*. You're looking for a place to stay?

KRIS. No, I'm staying at the zoo.

SUSAN. I've never met anyone who lived at the zoo before.

FRED. The zoo is no place to stay. Why don't you stay with me. I've got an extra bed in my apartment, and I could use some company.

KRIS. Well, thank you, Mr. Gayley. That's very nice of you... Susan, maybe you should go and tell your mother that we have made an arrangement. I don't want her to worry about me.

SUSAN. Okay, Mr. Kringle, I like the idea of your staying with Fred. He's my friend, and it's right next door.

KRIS & FRED. Good night, Susan. *(SUSAN exits.)*

KRIS. I like the idea, too, Mr. Gayley.

FRED. Call me Fred, please.

KRIS. All right, Fred. Staying so close by will give me more opportunity to work on Susan's Christmas gift.

FRED. I'm really very fond of that little girl.

KRIS. I can see that... And how about her mother?

FRED *(pauses, sighs)*. I really like her, but I'm afraid she feels that being neighbors, and baby sitter with Susan, is as close as she wants me to get.

KRIS. Have you ever invited her out?

FRED. I've tried. But Doris won't socialize since her divorce. She just concentrates on Susan and her career. I don't think she trusts love anymore.

KRIS. An old, sad story... But it's one that maybe you and I can do something about, Fred.

FRED *(cheers up)*. Oh, yeah? How do we start?

KRIS. It's simple. Just keep showing your interest in her, and be aware of her feelings. Above all, you must have faith in her.

FRED. I've tried all that. It hasn't done any good so far.

KRIS *(smiling brightly)*. Things will work out. I'll see to that.

(DORIS re-enters.)

DORIS. Mr. Kringle, Ms. Shellhammer has a place for you to stay. And she lives right near the store, so you can get to work easily. Is that okay? I'll call a cab, and you can go right now.

KRIS. That's very thoughtful of her. But I've just accepted Mr. Gayley's offer to stay with him.

DORIS. Mr. Gayley? *(FRED nods innocently.)* I see.

KRIS. I hope you don't mind. *(DORIS doesn't know what to say.)* Well, then, if you'll excuse me, I'll go and get my things from the zoo. I'll be back soon… *(Starts to exit.)*

DORIS. Wait, I'll get you a cab.

KRIS. Oh, don't bother. There will be one right outside, thank you.

DORIS *(after KRIS is gone)*. I should tell you about him, Fred. I don't suppose you realize he's been diagnosed as suffering from delusions. Kris's doctor has asked me to keep an eye on him. He should not be left unsupervised.

FRED. Aside from the fact that I think he's quite capable of handling himself, he'll only be next door. Between the two of us, we should have the situation covered.

DORIS. Well, that's not quite all.

FRED. Oh?

DORIS. The Santa Claus bit. I don't want Susan influenced. I thought I had made that clear to you.

FRED. I understand your concerns, Doris. But I like Kris. Why not try it out for a couple of days, and if the arrangement doesn't work, we'll find another place for him. In the meantime, I'll take responsibility for him. Trust me, Doris… Deal? *(He holds out his hand.)*

DORIS *(reluctantly, realizing she's stuck)*. Well...okay.

(They shake. Blackout to indicate passage of time. A group of CAROLERS enters singing. KRIS enters carrying a suitcase, sees the CAROLERS and joins in. He moves away with them at the end of the song. Lights up again in Doris' apartment. A knock on the door. After a moment DORIS opens. FRED enters.)

DORIS. Hi. Is everything all right?

FRED. Did Kris come back here?

DORIS. No. Isn't he with you?

FRED. When he didn't show up, I went to the zoo to find him. The man told me he had already been there to get his things and left over an hour ago.

DORIS. Oh, heavens, Fred! Something's happened to him!

FRED. It's all my fault. And after I told you you could trust me.

DORIS. I don't want to blame you.

FRED. I shouldn't have let him go get his things by himself.

DORIS. The important thing now is to find out if he's all right. I'd never forgive myself if something happened to him.

FRED. I'm surprised. I didn't think you liked Kris.

DORIS. It's not a matter of like.

FRED. I was hoping this was a sign that what he stands for was getting to you.

DORIS. No. But this is New York City, you know.

FRED. Come on, Doris. Who's going to mug Santa Claus?

DORIS *(looks at him a moment)*. I'm calling the police. *(Picks up phone.)*

FRED. Look, Doris, if Kris can get here from the North Pole, then New York shouldn't be any problem for him.

DORIS. I'm serious, Fred. If he was all right, he would have called by now. He must know I'd be worried.

(She starts to dial. SUSAN enters from bedroom, sobbing, holding blanket. DORIS puts phone down.)

DORIS. Why, what's wrong, sweetheart?

SUSAN. I dreamed that Mr. Kringle went away and there wasn't any more Christmas.

DORIS. Susan, you know that dreams aren't real.

FRED *(has taken SUSAN beside him on the sofa)*. It was only a dream, Susan. Mr. Kringle will be fine. And we'll never lose Christmas as long as we have each other. *(He sings a lullaby or soothing Christmas carol, and SUSAN falls asleep.)*

DORIS *(watching the peaceful scene)*. I don't know what I would have done without you tonight, Fred. I don't think I have ever shown my appreciation for your friendship and the way you care for Susan… Please forgive me for…getting so upset with you… *(She breaks up.)*

FRED *(pulls her down on the sofa with him and SUSAN)*. Thank you. Thank you for opening up to me.

DORIS. I…uh… *(Sob.)*

FRED. Thanks for recognizing that I'm right here with you. *(They lean toward each other in anticipation of a kiss.)*

(KRIS opens door, stops on seeing them.)

KRIS. Oh, excuse me. I'll come back at a more convenient time.

DORIS *(jumps up)*. Kris! You're back. *(She runs to hug him.)*

FRED. Where were you? We've been very worried. *(Gets up from sofa, SUSAN wakes up.)*

KRIS. Just singing carols with some of my friends. I just came by to say good night.

DORIS. I'm so relieved!

SUSAN. Then my dream was true. Santa really did go away.

FRED. But he came back because your mother cared about him.

DORIS. That's a nice thought, anyway. Everything is all right now, Susan. Come on, I'll tuck you back in bed.

FRED. Good night again, Susan. *(DORIS and SUSAN exit.)*

KRIS *(with significance to FRED)*. Did you enjoy my absence?

FRED. What do you mean? Doris was nearly crazy with worry.

KRIS. Didn't it bring the two of you closer together?

FRED. Well, yes.

KRIS. That's exactly what I hoped would happen.

FRED. You old fox! You worried us on purpose! You ought to he ashamed of yourself!

KRIS. Not a bit. Now, let me get out of here so you can finish putting her worries to rest.

(DORIS re-enters.)

FRED *(handing KRIS the key to his apartment)*. Here. It's the next door on the right. I'm really happy that you're staying with me, Kris. But I confess, I have an ulterior motive.

KRIS. Oh? What's that?

FRED. I'm finally going to learn the answer to the question that has plagued the world for centuries: Does Santa sleep with his whiskers inside or outside the covers?

KRIS *(laughs)*. I always sleep with 'em out. Cold air makes 'em grow... Now, I'll find my way, thank you. *(Exits with a wink to FRED.)*

DORIS. Believe it or not, I'm glad he's staying at your place. I feel better about having him safe and near. I'm glad you're near too.

FRED. Me too. *(Coming close, they kiss.)*

SCENE SIX

SCENE: *Macy's Toy Department, Santa's dais. One week later. Elf Theater optional.*

SHELLHAMMER. And now, ladies and gentlemen, a special Christmas delight: Macy's ~~Elf Theater~~! *Elves*

(ELVES perform. KRIS watches from his "throne.")

SHELLHAMMER. And now, a very special honor: Mr. Macy, Mr. Bloomingdale.

(MACY and BLOOMINGDALE step to DC.)

MACY *(to BLOOMINGDALE)*. Welcome to our store. I'm so happy that we can work together in the spirit of Christmas. *(They shake hands. Photographers' bulbs flash.)*
Take picture

BLOOMINGDALE. Yes, I must admit, I was at first very jealous of the popularity of your goodwill campaign. I felt you were stealing Christmas business from us. Then someone reminded me that goodwill isn't any organization's private property. So we started our own goodwill operation. I must say, it has been most profitable for us.

MACY. That's right. Goodwill goes a lot farther with everybody than competition. Now, would you come forward, Mr. Kringle? *(KRIS joins them. To BLOOMINGDALE.)*

This is the man I told you about. *(To KRIS.)* Mr. Kringle, you have brought a very special spirit to both Macy's and Bloomingdale's stores this Christmas season. And it seems to have spread to the entire city of New York as well. Whatever your special gift, it deserves recognition and appreciation. In honor of your distinguished service, Macy's would like to present to you this token of our esteem and gratitude. *(He hands a check to KRIS.)*

KRIS *(glances at check).* Oh, thank you so much. This is very generous... It's going to make Christmas really special for someone who has been kind to me... It's going to buy an X-ray machine.

MACY. A what?

KRIS. It's for the medical facility at the Maplewood Home. Doctor Pierce says an X-ray is very helpful in some situations.

MACY. That's going to he quite expensive. That check won't...

BLOOMINGDALE. Let me handle it for you. We'll get it for you wholesale.

MACY *(not to be outdone).* We'll get it for you at *cost!*

KRIS. Thank you both very much. *(He shakes hands with MACY and BLOOMINGDALE as photographers' bulbs flash again.)*

BLOOMINGDALE *(pointing at photographers).* Will you folks, and you too, Mr. Macy, and Mr. Kringle... Will you come over to Bloomingdale's to take some more pictures in front of my store? *(To KRIS.)* And since you have brought extra business to Bloomingdale's, there will be a bonus check for you there. That should help pay for that expensive machine. *(Exit ALL, ad libbing cheerful words. DORIS and FRED are left.)*

DORIS. Pinch me, Fred. I simply don't believe it. I never thought I'd see Mr. Macy shake hands with Mr. Bloomingdale! It's surely a miracle.

FRED. I don't know how he does it.

DORIS. Who?

FRED. Kris.

DORIS. Maybe he gathered some stardust while he was sailing through the air with his reindeer and sprinkled it on everybody.

FRED. Doris! You're imagination is coming to life!

DORIS. Not really, Fred. I was only kidding.

FRED. No, you weren't. Don't be afraid to admit it. And here. I have a little presentation of my own to make. *(He takes a small box from his pocket.)*

DORIS. What is it? *(She opens the box and removes a necklace.)* Oh, Fred... It's beautiful!

FRED. Here, let me... *(He fastens necklace on her.)* I went to Cartiers to look at necklaces, and you know what they did? They sent me to Tiffany's. Then the clerk at Tiffany's asked me if I'd seen the collection at Cartiers.

DORIS. It's happening all over town! I never dreamed, when I saw that jolly bearded man at the parade, that he would revolutionize the entire merchandising business.

FRED. Let's celebrate and have dinner together.

DORIS. Fred, I'd really love to, but I have to work tonight.

FRED *(disappointed)*. Really?

DORIS. Really. Unfortunately, it's been planned for weeks. Mr. Sawyer, our vocational guidance counselor, has a lecture this evening for our employees.

FRED. Can't you get out of it?

DORIS. I'm sorry, no. I have to introduce him.

FRED. What's the topic? *(DORIS and FRED start walking away.)*

DORIS. This is embarrassing. *(She accidentally drops invitation card as she goes.)* Please don't mention it to Kris... *(They exit together.)*

(A couple of ELVES enter. One of them picks up card and reads.)

ELF Q. "...Exploding the myth of Santa Claus"? "Open discussion following lecture"? Oh, dear, we'll have to show *this* to Mr. Kringle!

SCENE SEVEN

SCENE: *Employee meeting room. That evening.*

DORIS is at lectern on the podium. SAWYER and SHELLY are sitting on each side of her.

DORIS. ...And so it gives me great pleasure to introduce Mr. Albert Sawyer.

SAWYER. Ladies and gentlemen, tonight we are here to explore the nature of the Santa Claus myth. By the time this lecture is concluded, I feel confident that you will share my heart-felt convictions that this legend, which has been handed down over the centuries, is an outrageous atrocity, and that it has been detrimental to generation after generation of innocent young persons of both genders. The symbolic figure of Santa Claus...

(KRIS and ELVES enter at rear of hall.)

SAWYER. ...St. Nicholas, or Kris Kringle, whatever we may call him, represents a classic expression of the wishful dreaming of all children. Instead of teaching children that things they want come for free, they should be taught, while they are still in their formative years, the value of the work ethic that has made this country great. They must realize that this is a hard and competitive world, and if they are to succeed, they must learn the difference between myth and reality. Mature adults who continue to perpetrate this fable reveal themselves as incomplete and neurotic personalities who have failed to adjust to the stringent demands of our culture. Not only have they damaged their own existence, but they are harming their children's future. A child who does not understand this marked difference between fact and fiction will grow up still clinging to infantile fantasies and never be able to face the cruel truths of today's world. *(DORIS winces.)* Why do we do this to ourselves, you ask?

KRIS *(aside)*. Don't ask!

SAWYER. To compensate for feelings of guilt. That's why we perpetuate the myth of Santa Claus. Parents who feel guilty because they've neglected their children 364 days of the year and pick this one day to overwhelm the kiddies with gifts, are doing it so as to purge their shameful behavior. And parents and grandparents who swamp the child with talk about Santa and stage the Christmas charade, are re-enacting their own infantile emotions which they have never outgrown. Therefore, I suspect that the vaunted "spirit of giving" is nothing but selfishness in disguise. *(ELVES boo and hiss.)* Far from doing any good in the world, this vicious myth has done more harm than...than...

KRIS *(beside himself with anger)*. Now just a minute, there! *(He starts toward the podium.)*

SAWYER. *I'm* giving this lecture, Mr. Kringle.

KRIS. An open discussion was to be included, I believe.

SAWYER. The discussion will take place after the lecture is over.

ELVES. The lecture *is* over! Boooooooo! We don't want to hear any more of this!

SAWYER *(turning to DORIS)*. Mrs. Walker, I refuse to continue... *(ELVES cheer)* ...until this blatant fraud is removed from the platform.

DORIS. Kris...we have to... Please...

KRIS. I'm sorry, Mrs. Walker, but I just can't sit here and listen to the depressing absurdity of this man's propaganda!

SAWYER. Absurdity, huh?... *(Advancing ominously toward KRIS.)*

KRIS. Fraud, am I... *(Taps his cane on palm of his hand.)*

SAWYER. Don't you try to threaten me... Mrs. Walker, I told you he would get violent... Stop!... *(KRIS stands holding his cane in front of himself for protection, as SAWYER moves toward him. SAWYER comes in contact with cane.)* See! *He hit me!*

KRIS. I did no such thing!

DORIS *(stepping between them)*. Let's calm down here, *Albert!...Kris!*

SAWYER. Now, look here, Mrs. Walker!... Are you going to allow this dangerous maniac to assault your employees?

DORIS. He's quite harmless, Mr. Sawyer.

SAWYER. Maybe we should let the police decide that!

DORIS *(in a dulcet voice)*. That concludes our meeting for this evening, ladies and gentlemen. Thank you so much for coming. And a Merry Christmas to you all... *(As audience supposedly files out chattering, she says firmly to KRIS.)* I'll handle this!

KRIS. I'm perfectly capable of defending my person against attacks, Mrs. Walker.

DORIS. Please, Kris…for my sake…

KRIS. All right…I'll see you at the store tomorrow. *(Starts to leave.)*

DORIS. No, Kris, would you wait in the hall, please? I'll talk to you in a minute. *(KRIS and ELVES exit.)*

SAWYER *(yelling after KRIS as he leaves)*. Society has ways of dealing with your kind! *(To DORIS.)* That's what I mean. He's a dangerously deranged man. In cases like this there is no warning… He could strike at any time.

DORIS. I hardly think…

SHELLHAMMER *(to DORIS)*. This could really backfire on Macy's. If Bloomingdale's, or the press, should find out that our Santa is…possibly…uh…dangerous, the repercussions could be devastating.

SAWYER. I'm telling you, Mrs. Walker, Kringle is a stick of dynamite with a short fuse. I warned you! Thank goodness I was the victim of his lunacy and not some poor, defenseless child dangling on his knee.

SHELLHAMMER. We've got to do something at once.

DORIS. But he's just a kindly old man. Are you sure he touched you with that cane?

SAWYER. Yes, and he will again! He has evidently suffered a sudden change of personality and has entered a violent stage!

DORIS. But Doctor Pierce assured me that such a thing could never happen with Kris. He said his delusion is a positive one.

SAWYER. Doctor Pierce is not a psychiatrist.

DORIS. Neither are you!

SAWYER. In that case, your responsibility is to have him thoroughly examined by a competent psychiatrist at once.

SHELLHAMMER. I agree.

DORIS. Well, I don't. Kris has been examined many times, according to Doctor Pierce.

SHELLHAMMER. Then one more time won't make any difference... If the psychiatrist finds him competent, then he can come right back and resume his job.

SAWYER. And if he doesn't, then you certainly will have done the right thing.

DORIS. Well, I...

SAWYER. The only problem now is to get him out of here without creating another scene. In his present condition, he would most certainly react with violence.

SHELLHAMMER. You'll have to explain it to him, Doris. He trusts you.

DORIS. I simply can't hurt the old man.

SAWYER. Well, never mind. I won't need you, Mrs. Walker. I know what to do.

DORIS. What are you going to do?

SAWYER. I'll apologize, and I'll invite him for dinner, and then persuade him to have an examination by a competent psychiatrist tomorrow.

DORIS. Well...all right, Albert... Call me later and let me know how you worked it out, okay?

SAWYER. Mr. Kringle, are you still there?

(KRIS re-enters, ELVES following.)

SAWYER. Please come back. I'm truly sorry about our misunderstanding. Are you all right? *(KRIS nods.)* I shouldn't have said the things I did. Could we have dinner together? Then I'd be happy to drop you off where you're staying.

KRIS. Well, certainly, Mr. Sawyer. I accept your apology. Thank you for the dinner invitation, but I believe I'll go with Mrs. Walker.

DORIS. That's all right, Kris. It'll give me time to take care of some shopping. I'll go with Ms. Shellhammer, and I'll see you in the morning. *(They exit.)*

SAWYER. Shall we go?

KRIS *(pauses)*. Would you excuse me a moment? I need to talk to the elves.

SAWYER. Of course. I'll just go collect my things. *(Exits.)*

KRIS *(to ELVES)*. I've been thinking. Do you remember how we should always look for the good in everyone, no matter how bad the person seems to be?

ELF R *(unbelieving)*. Does "everyone" include Mr. Sawyer?

KRIS. Sometimes the good in people is buried so deep that it has a difficult time trying to get out. When it does come out, we may not be able to recognize it because we've blocked off our willingness to see it. Mr. Sawyer sees things very narrowly because he lacks the ability to dream. That means he can't imagine anything being better than his limited view.

ELF W. Is there hope for him?

KRIS. Of course there is. He just apologized for his angry words. I don't know if he was sincere…but still, we must encourage his good feelings in every way we can.

ELF R. What if he wasn't being honest?

KRIS. That would mean…that the bad was, *at the moment*, stronger than the good.

ELF W. You shouldn't go with him, Mr. Kringle!

KRIS. Not so fast. We must be quick to recognize the good intentions in his words. Having said them, even he, deep down, believes he should mean them.

ELF Q. I'm calling for a vote of the elves on whether Mr.
Kringle should go with Mr. Sawyer. All those in favor?

KRIS. Aye!

ELF Q. Opposed?

ELVES *(shouting)*. Opposed!

KRIS. I'm sorry, but I'm in charge of me. So the ayes have
it. I'm going to give Mr. Sawyer a chance. Besides, it's
Mrs. Walker who decided I should go with him. Don't
worry. I can take care of myself. You elves go on home,
and I'll see you in the morning.

ELVES. If you say so, sir. But please be careful.

(ELVES ad lib as they file out. SAWYER enters.)

KRIS. Oh, there you are, Mr. Sawyer. Where shall we go to
have dinner?

SCENE EIGHT

SCENE: *Bellevue State Hospital, Men's Ward.*

*KRIS is dressed in a shroud-like gown, sitting dejectedly
on his bed. FRED stands beside him.*

KRIS. How could she have done it? How could she have
done this to me?

FRED. Doris didn't send you here. She thought Sawyer was
taking you to dinner.

KRIS *(not really hearing him)*. She must have been humoring
me all along. I thought she was beginning to believe in me.

FRED. How did it happen that you went with him to Bellevue?

KRIS. He tricked me. Sawyer kept looking out of the restaurant window as he made small talk. Suddenly he said, "Let's go," and when I stepped outside he pushed me into a waiting taxi, and two men put me between them. Then I heard one of them say "Bellevue." Sawyer didn't even come along.

FRED. Didn't they give you the usual sanity tests that you know by heart?

KRIS. Of course, the same routine. But I was so crushed that Doris would do this to me that I deliberately gave them all the wrong answers. So they committed me.

FRED. Doris had no idea what Sawyer was up to, Kris. She agreed that you two would have dinner and he would only talk with you about seeing a psychiatrist.

KRIS. I'm relieved to know that. But why didn't she come to me herself and explain?

FRED. She was afraid of hurting you, Kris.

KRIS. Well, it hurt anyway. I'm just a nice old man she felt sorry for.

FRED. She feels more than that, I'm sure.

KRIS *(shakes his head)*. No... She had doubts, Fred. That's why she isn't here. If *you* had been dragged off here, she would have been here in a heartbeat.

FRED. She certainly had doubts at first. But, she was really beginning to open up and believe. I think her belief was still too new and fragile, and Sawyer may have tipped her the other way. Kris, I'm sure that Doris won't want you to stay here.

KRIS. It's not just Doris. It's people like Sawyer. He's dishonest and... Ohhhh...I don't want to say the other awful words that occur to me... Yet he's the one who's called normal. If that's how sane people behave, then I'd rather stay here with these more honest folks.

FRED. Nonsense, Kris! You're quite sane, and a whole lot saner than most.

KRIS. Yet he's out there, and I'm in here. I should have listened to the elves. I believed there was some good in that man that I could touch. Now I'll be spending my life at Mt. Hope after all, the way Doctor Pierce said.

FRED. Kris! Don't be so gloomy! You're not living up to your own philosophy. You can't just think of yourself.

KRIS. Eh?... Am I just thinking of myself?

FRED. You can't give up! What happens to you matters to a whole lot of people. People like me who have faith in you and what you stand for. And people like Susan who are just beginning to learn about faith.

KRIS *(hesitantly, then building)*. Well... Maybe... Maybe you're right... Maybe you're right, at that... I should be ashamed of myself. And by golly I am!... Come on, Fred! Let's get out of here!

FRED. *Wait* a minute there, Kris. It's not that easy. *(Doubtful.)* There are some legal matters that may be difficult to clear up. I'm not sure...

KRIS. You tell *me* not to be discouraged. Now, don't *you* be discouraged... I've got faith in you, Fred. I know you'll be able to do it.

FRED. Really? Then I'll *do* it! I'll get you out of here! *(They shake hands.)*

END OF ACT ONE

ACT TWO

SCENE ONE

enter SR

SCENE: *Judge's chambers, one week later.*

JUDGE HARPER is sitting at his desk. FINLEY, the bailiff, enters.

FINLEY. Good morning, what a beautiful day. And it's been a good year for you too, hasn't it, Your Honor?

JUDGE. Yes, things have gone pretty well. I see no reason why the spring election won't fall in my lap. Perhaps my Christmas present to Mrs. Harper ought to be more elaborate this year...maybe that trip to Bermuda.

FINLEY. Oh, that ought to be real nice, sir. Uh...Ms. Mara from the attorney general's office is here to see you, Your Honor.

JUDGE. Ahh good. Show her in. *(FINLEY exits.)* *exit SL*

(MARA enters with folders in hand. They are old friends; they exchange greetings.)

MARA. Just some routine commitment papers, Your Honor. *(Puts them on desk.)* You'll find everything in order. *(JUDGE leafs through thick file.)* I've checked them over carefully. The psychiatric report from Bellevue Hospital is attached.

JUDGE. Bellevue, eh? *(Reading.)* Age...unknown. An old man, huh?

54

MARA. Very old, Your Honor.

JUDGE *(with a sigh)*. I suppose I should read all this.

MARA. You can take my word for it… It's a clear-cut consent proceeding. This fellow calls himself Kris Kringle. He thinks he's Santa Claus.

JUDGE. Uh-oh. *(Chuckles.)*

(FINLEY enters.)   enter SL

FINLEY. A Mr. Gayley to see you, Your Honor.

JUDGE. What does he want?

FINLEY. He said he's representing a person named Kris Kringle, sir.

JUDGE. Better show him in. *(To MARA.)* Santa Claus has a lawyer?

(FINLEY admits FRED.)   up SL, stand

FINLEY. Right this way, sir. *(Exits.)*

FRED. Good afternoon, Your Honor. My name is Fred Gayley, I represent Mr. Kringle. I believe you have received the papers.

JUDGE. Yes, just a matter of signing the consent, it seems. That'll get the old fellow out of harm's way for what's left of his life.

FRED. No, if you don't mind, Your Honor. There are indications that Mr. Kringle has been victimized, and I have requested a proper hearing so that I can provide witnesses.

JUDGE *(to MARA)*. I thought you said this case was clear cut.

MARA. It was, as far as I knew. This is the first I've heard about a challenge.

JUDGE. This psychiatric evaluation, Mr. Gayley. There is a clear diagnosis… *(Thumbing through more papers.)* And here is a statement saying that in addition to his delusion, he became violent. That seems like a pretty clear basis for commitment, don't you think?

FRED. That is a misrepresentation, Your Honor. That's why I'm requesting a hearing.

JUDGE *(ponders)*. I'm thinking about court time and expense to the taxpayers, Mr. Gayley.

FRED. Your Honor may sign the commitment papers, if you wish, sir, but I must advise you, I will submit a writ of habeas corpus.

JUDGE. That won't be necessary. We might as well have a competency hearing. *(Looks at his calendar.)* Let's see… Next Monday morning. Ten o'clock. Is that all right with you?

FRED. Fine. And thank you, Your Honor. *(Exits.)*

JUDGE. Ms. Mara?

MARA. Just when I thought I was getting my calendar cleared for a Christmas vacation… Yes, Your Honor, I'll work it in.

JUDGE. See you on Monday, then. *(MARA exits.)*

MARA *(as she passes FINLEY)*. Have a good day, Finley.

FINLEY. Thank you, ma'am, the same to you.

(SAWYER rushes up to FINLEY.)   stop Sawyer

SAWYER. Whom do I see about dropping the Kringle commitment case?

MARA *(overhears, stops)*. Kringle's commitment has been challenged, Mr.…ah…

SAWYER. Sawyer.

MARA. Yes. His certification of insanity is unequivocal. But wouldn't you know, even Bellevue's word isn't good enough.

SAWYER. I'd like this case to be dropped right away. Isn't there anything we can do?

MARA. Sorry. The hearing is scheduled for next Monday morning.

SAWYER. A public hearing! Attorneys! Mr. Macy has demanded that I get Santa Claus back. This is disastrous!

MARA. Oh, don't worry. This kid, Gayley, Kringle's lawyer, is just a young sport trying to get himself a little publicity.

SAWYER. Publicity! My job...gone! No Christmas bonus!... *(As he heads off stage.)* Maybe Mrs. Walker can talk to Mr. Gayley...

(Radio broadcast is heard during blackout.)

NEWSCASTER. Good evening, folks. This is Sidney Stewart on your New York News Station, WZYX. Today's top story from New York City is the controversial sanity hearing of... You won't believe this... Kris Kringle, also known as: You guessed it—Santa Claus. It seems that Macy's St. Nick says he IS the real Santa Claus, and the state of New York wants to put him away for saying so. This could result in a lot of disappointed children and empty stockings on Christmas morning. We'll keep you informed on what happens to Santa in the New York judicial system as the hearing progresses.

SCENE TWO

SCENE: *Judge's chamber.*

HALLORAN *(approaches judge's chamber).* Hello, Finley. Is the judge in?

(FINLEY responds affirmatively and HALLORAN enters.)

HALLORAN. Hello, Henry, how are you? *(He doesn't wait for an answer.)* Henry, you know I've been a good friend of yours for years, as well as your political manager. Now, we've been successful in keeping you on this bench, haven't we?

JUDGE. Yes, yes. Of course, Charlie. I'm very grateful to you. I like this seat and hope to keep it a while.

HALLORAN. All right. We've got elections coming up in the spring. Right?

JUDGE. I'm ready, Charlie. Is there any problem?

HALLORAN. Henry, I've been reading the papers. Seriously, are you going to have... *(Incredulous.)* Santa Claus...in your courtroom?

JUDGE *(chortles).* Is there something you'd like me to ask him to bring you for Christmas?

HALLORAN. No, Henry. I'd like to give *you* a Christmas present. How about a trip—a vacation. Now! Take Madeleine and escape to Bermuda as you've been talking about.

JUDGE. I'd like to, but I won't be able to get away very soon. My calendar's too full.

HALLORAN. No, I mean right away. You look a little run-down to me, Henry. You ought to take a few weeks off.

JUDGE. Nonsense. I never felt better in my life.

HALLORAN. Go fishing... Go hiking... Go *anywhere!*...

JUDGE. Why should I?

HALLORAN. Because this Santa Claus case is explosive, Henry. You've got to get out of it somehow.

JUDGE. I can't just walk out on a case. It's all arranged.

HALLORAN. Then have a sudden illness. Let another judge handle it...somebody who isn't coming up for re-election right away.

JUDGE. Hey, Charlie, relax. I'm an honest man. I wouldn't fake an illness. And maybe the Santa Claus case will be some good publicity for the campaign.

HALLORAN. Good publicity? You'd become a regular Pontius Pilate before you even start the campaign! You'll be a villain to every little kid who believes in Santa Claus.

JUDGE. They don't vote.

HALLORAN. But their parents do. Any father or mother who has to explain to the kid why "Santa Claus" went to jail is going to hate you.

JUDGE. Not jail. State hospital.

HALLORAN. Same thing! Wake up, Henry!

(Optional. Interim action. Street corner, waiting for signal to change.)

1ST PEDESTRIAN *(to pedestrian next to him)*. Did you see this thing about trying Santa Claus for sanity?

2ND PEDESTRIAN. Yeah, I saw it. I think the guy's crazy, don't you?

3RD PEDESTRIAN. What was that? I didn't here about it.

2ND PEDESTRIAN. Yeah. This fellow calls himself Kris Kringle. Gotta be nuts.

3RD PEDESTRIAN. Oh, I don't know. Why shouldn't there be a real Santa Claus? I think it's a nice idea.

1ST PEDESTRIAN. Even if he isn't real, I just hope they don't put the old guy away. He's no harm to anybody. *(Signal changes, and they go their ways.)*

SCENE THREE

enter SR

SCENE: *Judge Harper's courtroom.*

FINLEY. Hear ye! Hear ye! All rise. The New York State Court is now in session. The Honorable Henry X. Harper presiding.

(JUDGE enters.)

JUDGE. Please be seated. *(ALL sit.)* Let us proceed.

MARA *(coming forward).* As the competency report has already been submitted in evidence, Your Honor, the prosecution wishes to call its first witness: Mr. Kris Kringle.

KRIS *(walks brightly to the witness stand).* Good morning, Your Honor. *(JUDGE smiles and nods, feeling a liking for the old guy.)*

FINLEY. Raise your right hand. Do you swear to tell the truth, the whole truth and nothing but the truth, so help you God?

KRIS. I do.

MARA. Please state your name for the record.

KRIS. Kris Kringle.

MARA. And where do you live?

KRIS. That's what this hearing will decide, I believe. *(MARA scowls. Courtroom chuckles.)*

JUDGE. A very sound answer, Mr. Kringle.

MARA. Do you believe that you are Santa Claus?

KRIS. Of course. *(Stunned silence.)*

MARA *(to JUDGE)*. The State rests its case, Your Honor.

(Courtroom reaction. HALLORAN catches JUDGE's attention.)

JUDGE *(to FRED, after nodding to HALLORAN)*. Well, young man, do you want to cross examine the witness? I believe he was employed to *play* Santa Claus. Perhaps he didn't understand the question.

KRIS. I understood it perfectly, Your Honor.

JUDGE. Uh… In view of the witness' statement, do you still wish to enter a defense, young man?

FRED. I do, Your Honor. I am fully aware that Mr. Kringle believes himself to he Santa Claus. In fact, that is the basis of the entire case against him. The State declares that this man is not sane just because he believes he is Santa Claus.

JUDGE. I believe that is a reasonable and logical premise for such a declaration, Mr. Gayley.

FRED. It would be, Your Honor, if you or I or Ms. Mara here, believed that we were Santa Claus.

MARA *(tartly)*. Anyone who thinks he is Santa Claus is out of touch with reality. Of course, he's insane!

FRED. Not necessarily. *(Significant pause.)* You believe yourself to be Judge Harper, Your Honor, and nobody questions your sanity, because you *are* Judge Harper.

JUDGE *(suspicious)*. I know all about myself, young man. Mr. Kringle is the subject of this hearing.

FRED. I was only making a point, Your Honor.

JUDGE. And your point is…?

FRED. I wished to clarify that if a person *is* the person he believes himself to be—just as you are, sir—then he is just as sane.

JUDGE. Of course. But he isn't.

FRED. Oh, but he *is*, Your Honor.

JUDGE. Is…WHAT?

FRED. I intend to prove that Mr. Kringle IS Santa Claus! *(Hubbub in courtroom. Flashbulbs. Reporters flee to call in stories to their editors. JUDGE bangs gavel for order.)*

JUDGE. This hearing is adjourned until tomorrow morning at ten a.m. *(Gavel.)*

SCENE FOUR

SCENE: *Restaurant, that evening.*

DORIS. I've read the evening paper, Fred, and I'm worried. You seem to be fighting such a hopeless battle.

FRED. Actually, I'm rather confident. All the publicity is working for us. Public sympathy is obviously behind Kris. I think we have a good chance.

DORIS. What about your law firm. How are they going to react to your taking this case?

FRED. Well actually, old Hayslip, the senior partner, called me in this afternoon. *(Mimics.)* "We are an old, established firm with great prestige and dignity, Mr. Gayley. We can't have one of our junior members making a public spectacle of himself. We are not in business to prove that some old crank is actually Santa Claus." In other words, unless I drop the case, they'll drop me.

DORIS. Well, then. You'll have to give it up, won't you?

FRED. I can't let a client down. You wouldn't want me to walk out on Kris, would you?

DORIS. Fred, I really care very deeply for you. I admire and respect you for your courage in taking this on. But I don't want to see you lose your position.

FRED. It's true. I might.

DORIS. That would be irresponsible. People have to he realistic. I've certainly learned that! You can't give up your job for some sentimental whim.

FRED. It's more than a whim, Doris.

DORIS. Stop dreaming, Fred!

FRED. There's something very beautiful about that old man, and very compelling, too. Representing Kris is the right thing to do, Doris. I *won't* let him down... And I'm a damned good lawyer, too. Come on, Doris, have faith in me.

DORIS *(angry)*. I do...but... It's not a question of having faith. You're bound to lose this case. That's just common sense.

FRED. Doris, faith is believing in something when common sense tells you not to. Your problem is that you've got too much common sense.

DORIS *(really angry now)*. It's a good thing one of us has! It's quite an asset, sometimes!

FRED. Can't you get over being afraid? Just let yourself believe in people...people like Kris...in laughter and joy and love and all the other intangibles.

DORIS. You can't pay the rent with intangibles.

FRED. And you can't live a life without them. *(They stare at each other.)* At least I can't. I thought Kris and I had broken through your armor, Doris. I hoped you would be ready to be more open-minded and open-hearted. *(DORIS turns away from him.)* Well...there's no use talking. We don't have many thoughts or feelings in common, do we?

DORIS. I suppose not.

FRED. Then there's nothing more to say.

DORIS *(preparing to leave)*. It's ironic... With all my common sense, I thought it was really going to work out this time.

FRED. So did I.

DORIS. Good-bye, Fred. *(Exits as FRED looks after her.)*

SCENE FIVE

SCENE: *Courtroom, the following day.*

FRED. As my first witness I call R.H. Macy.

(MACY takes the stand.)

FINLEY *(to MR. MACY)*. Do you swear to tell the truth, the whole truth, and nothing but the truth, so help you God?

MACY. I do.

FRED. Are you Mr. R.H. Macy, owner of one of the largest department stores in New York City?

MACY. Yes, and fifty-one stores nationwide.

FRED. Right. And is Mr. Kringle one of your employees?

MACY. Yes.

FRED. Do you believe him to be sane?

MACY. Definitely.

FRED. Do you believe him to be truthful?

MARA *(jumping up)*. Remember, you are under oath, Mr. Macy.

JUDGE. Ms. Mara, you will have a chance to cross-examine the witness after Mr. Gayley is finished.

FRED. Perhaps I can ask Ms. Mara's question for her. Mr. Macy, do you believe this man to be Santa Claus?

MACY *(hesitates, gulps, then answers in a large, defiant voice)*. YES!

FRED. No further questions.

JUDGE. Ms. Mara, do you wish to... *(MARA shakes her head. To MACY.)* You may step down.

MACY *(as he returns to his seat, points at SAWYER in the audience)*. You're fired! *(SAWYER rushes from scene.)*

FRED. As my next witness I call Doctor Pierce.

FINLEY. Doctor Pierce please take the stand. *(PIERCE takes* ~~Repeat~~ *stand.)* Do you swear to tell the truth, the whole truth, and nothing but the truth, so help you God?

PIERCE. I do.

FRED. Doctor Pierce, you are the resident physician at the Maplewood Home, are you not? *(PIERCE responds affirmatively.)* And you have known Kris Kringle for many years. Is that right? *(PIERCE nods.)* Do you believe him to be Santa Claus?

PIERCE *(softly)*. Yes.

FRED. Would you mind saying that louder, Doctor. I want the court to hear you.

PIERCE. Yes, I do.

MARA. Doctor, you are a man of science, are you not? Have you any rational, scientific reasons for your opinion?

JUDGE. Ms. Mara, I must caution you again! You may question the witness when Mr. Gayley is finished.

MARA. Yes, Your Honor.

FRED. Doctor Pierce, did you express a Christmas wish to Mr. Kringle several weeks ago?

PIERCE. Yes.

FRED. What was it?

PIERCE. Well, I wanted an X-ray machine for the medical facility at the Maplewood Home.

FRED. And what arrived at Maplewood yesterday.

PIERCE. An X-ray machine.

FRED. Where did it come from?

PIERCE. The card said, "Merry Christmas from Kris Kringle."

FRED. Thank you, Doctor. *(To MARA.)* Your witness.

MARA. Doctor Pierce, lots of Christmas presents come with cards saying "From Santa Claus." Do you know of any other possible donors?

PIERCE. No.

MARA. Now, be careful, Doctor Pierce. We are in a court of law, and only tangible facts and logical testimony can be accepted as evidence...Tell the court, why do you feel so sure a very expensive item like this machine came from an old man who has just a temporary Christmas job in a department store?

PIERCE. Because he is the only one to whom I said anything about it. And when I expressed the wish, I said, "If I get this X-ray machine, I'll *know* you're really Santa Claus." And I got it, and I do. *(Courtroom reacts. MARA turns away in disgust.)*

JUDGE. Thank you. You may step down.

FRED. As my next witness I call Jim Duncan.

(DUNCAN takes the stand.)

FINLEY *(to DUNCAN)*. Do you swear to tell the truth, the whole truth, and nothing but the truth, so help you God?

DUNCAN. I do.

FRED. Mr. Duncan, you are a zookeeper at the Central Park zoo, are you not?

DUNCAN. Yes, I am.

FRED. Jim, tell us about Mr. Kringle.

DUNCAN. Kris has a wonderful way with the reindeer—it's uncanny. I'm the antelope man at the zoo—have been for years—but I have always had difficulty with reindeer. The only time I can get near them is when they are restrained. Yet these same reindeer will walk right up to Mr. Kringle and eat out of his hand.

MARA. Objection! This is irrelevant and immaterial—not to mention ridiculous. Mr. Gayley is making a circus out of this proceeding. Does he plan to have the reindeer testify, for heaven's sake? There is no such person as Santa Claus, Your Honor. Everybody knows it. *(ELVES boo, courtroom reacts.)*

JUDGE *(pounding gavel).* Order in the court! Order in the court!

FRED. Your Honor, may I ask Ms. Mara a question? All the witnesses have testified not only that there IS a Santa Claus, but that he is sitting in this courtroom. Can you offer any positive proof that there is *no* Santa Claus?

MARA. Well… No… Of course I can't! *(Stronger.)* And I don't intend to try! This isn't a nursery! This is a New York State Court! We are wasting the court's time with this childish nonsense. Is there, or is there not a Santa Claus? I ask His Honor for an immediate ruling. *(Immediate hubbub. HALLORAN and JUDGE signal each other. JUDGE pounds gavel.)*

JUDGE. The court will take a short recess to consider the matter.

FINLEY. All rise…

SCENE SIX

SCENE: *Judge's chambers.*

HALLORAN. Look here, Henry. I don't care what you decide about old whisker-puss out there, but if you officially
rule that there is no Santa Claus, you might just as well
start looking for a chicken ranch somewhere. We won't
even be able to put you in the primaries!

JUDGE. I'm a sane person and a responsible official. I've
taken an oath. How can I say there *is* a Santa Claus, Charlie? If I do they'll have me de-robed and try *me* for insanity!

HALLORAN. Listen, Henry. Do you know how many mil-
lions of dollars' worth of toys are produced each year?
Toys that wouldn't be sold if it weren't for Santa Claus?
Have you ever heard of the National Association of Manu-
facturers? How do you think they would like your ruling?
And how about all the people they employ to make those
toys? Union members, Henry! They're gonna love you!
And they're gonna say it with votes!... Then there are the
department stores...and the candy companies...and the
Christmas card artists and printers... And what about the
Salvation Army? They've got a Santa Claus on every corner, and it's their biggest source of income... I'm telling
you, Henry, if you rule that there's no Santa Claus, you
can count on getting just two votes: yours and that lawyer,
Mara's.

JUDGE *(shakes his head sadly, puts up one finger)*. One.
Mara's a Republican. *(He exits to courtroom.)*

SCENE SEVEN

SCENE: *Courtroom.*

FINLEY *(as JUDGE enters)*. All rise.

JUDGE *(after courtroom is seated)*. The question of Santa Claus is...uh...by and large a matter of opinion. Many people firmly believe in him. Many others do not. The tradition of American justice demands a broad and unprejudiced view of such a controversial matter. This court intends to keep an open mind. I will hear any evidence from either position. *(Courtroom reacts moderately.)*

FRED. Your Honor, I believe I have some further evidence. I call J. Mara to the stand.

MARA *(startled)*. Who? Me?

FRED. Miss Janet [or "Master James," if played by boy] Mara. *(JANET takes stand. To JUDGE.)* May we skip the oath, Your Honor? *(JUDGE nods.)* Now, do you believe in Santa Claus, Janet?

JANET. Sure I do. He brought me a doll buggy [sled] last year.

FRED. What does he look like?

JANET. He's sitting right over there!

MARA. Objection!

JUDGE. Overruled.

FRED. Tell me, Janet, why are you so sure there is a Santa Claus?

JANET. Because my mommy told me so. *(Outburst from crowd. JUDGE grins and raps for order.)*

FRED. And you believe your mommy, don't you, Janet? She's a truthful person.

JANET. Of course. My mommy wouldn't tell me something that wasn't so.

FRED. Thank you, Janet. You may go.

JANET *(as she passes KRIS)*. Don't forget a real beauty parlor set [official football helmet].

KRIS. You shall have it, Janet.

MARA *(gloomy)*. Your Honor, the state of New York concedes the existence of Santa Claus… But…having so conceded, Your Honor, we ask that Mr. Gayley cease presenting personal opinion as evidence. The State could bring in hundreds of witnesses with opposite opinions. It is our intention to shorten this hearing if possible. I therefore demand that Mr. Gayley submit *authoritative and tangible proof* that Mr. Kringle is *the one and only Santa Claus!*

JUDGE. A point well taken, Ms. Mara. I'm afraid I must agree.

FRED. Your Honor, I am not prepared to present "authoritative and tangible proof" at this time. May I ask for an adjournment until tomorrow?

JUDGE. The court stands adjourned until tomorrow afternoon at three. *(Gavel.)*

FINLEY. All rise.

SUSAN *(as everyone begins to leave)*. Is Mr. Kringle coming over tonight, Mother?

DORIS. I'm afraid not.

SUSAN. He hasn't come for so long.

DORIS. Susan, Mr. Kringle may never be able to come and see us again.

SUSAN. Why not?

DORIS. Well… It's because he says he's Santa Claus.

SUSAN. But he has to be Santa Claus. He's just like everything Santa is supposed to be. Nobody could be like Mr. Kringle except Santa Claus.

DORIS. I wish you were right. He's going to be very unhappy if people say he isn't Santa Claus.

SUSAN. Then I want to write him a letter to cheer him up. What's his address, Mother?

DORIS. I'm not sure where he's staying. But I know he'd get it if you sent it to the New York State Courthouse, New York City... Let's go home and I'll help you.

SCENE EIGHT

SCENE: *Mail room at NYC post office.*

AL. Here's a new one! They write to Santa Claus at the North Pole, the South Pole, care of the postmaster, and every other way. But this kid writes to Mr. Kris Kringle at the New York State Court! Special delivery, too.

LOU. The kid's right, you know. That's where he is. Don't you read the papers?

AL. Sure, I read the papers—the news I want to read, like the Mets and the San Francisco Giants are out of the playoffs.

LOU. They've got him on trial down there—this Kringle guy. He claims he's Santa Claus and some D.A. claims he's nuts.

AL. You mean there's a guy who really might be Santa Claus?

LOU. A lot of people think he is.

AL. Well, what's the matter with you, Lou? You ain't very bright today. This guy Kringle is the solution to our problem!

LOU. Geez! Why didn't I think of that!

AL. Order a special big truck! Order a couple of 'em! Get 'em up here right away! All this Santa Claus mail we got lying around here...

LOU. You got it, Al!

SCENE NINE

SCENE: *Judge's chambers.*

HALLORAN. Henry, the publicity on the Kringle hearing has reached massive proportions. They're writing blazing headlines about it.

JUDGE *(gloomy)*. Yeah. I've seen the papers too.

HALLORAN. So… What are you going to do? You have to think of your situation.

JUDGE. *And* my duty to my office.

HALLORAN. Today is Christmas Eve. If you send Santa Claus to the nut house on Christmas Eve, you're likely to be up for a protest demonstration…or assaulted…or even murdered!

JUDGE *(sighs)*. I know. It's desperate… If that young Gayley can figure out the slightest "competent authority" reference that I can use for a sanity ruling, I will willingly and eagerly give him every possible break. I've been observing Mr. Kringle very carefully. He seems to be nothing worse than a very kindly old gentleman. But…unless something miraculous happens, I'll have no alternative but to accept the report of incompetency and have the old guy put away. *(He exits toward courtroom, followed by HALLORAN.)*

SCENE TEN

SCENE: *Courtroom.*

Crowd is waiting for hearing to resume. SUSAN and DORIS are among the spectators. KRIS and FRED are in their places.

SUSAN. Oh, Mother, now that we're here, I'm getting scared. What if Mr. Gayley loses, and they send Mr. Kringle away? What if he *isn't* Santa Claus, just like you said?

DORIS. Susan, I probably wasn't right when I told you that. You must believe in Mr. Kringle—have faith in him.

SUSAN. Then you think I'll really get my Christmas wish?

DORIS *(looking at FRED)*. Faith is believing in things when common sense tells you not to. We have to believe, Susan, or we'll never get anything. You and I both have to.

SUSAN. I believe, I believe, I believe…

(KRIS is holding a letter.)

KRIS. Fred, listen to this! *(Reading aloud.)* "Dear Mr. Kringle: I miss you very much, and I hope I will see you soon. I know it will all come out all right. I believe you are Santa Claus, and I hope you are not sad. Yours truly, Susan Walker." And what's this? "P.S. I believe in you too. Love, Doris."

(FRED goes to DORIS—they embrace. A GUARD comes to FRED and whispers something. They leave courtroom.)

KRIS. Well, what do you know… Susan, come here, dear.

SUSAN *(going to him and hugging him)*. Mr. Kringle, I believe.

KRIS. Thank you for your letter, Susan. No matter how this hearing ends, I know that my efforts have not been in vain.

SUSAN. It will come out all right. I just know it, because I believe in you.

(SUSAN returns to her seat. FRED re-enters, grinning confidently. He holds a large book.)

KRIS *(holding up SUSAN's letter).* Fred, wait till you see this letter!

FRED. Hold on to your hat, Kris. You ain't seen nothin' yet!

(Lights up on whole scene as JUDGE enters.)

FINLEY. All rise. *(ALL stand, then sit as JUDGE sits.)*

JUDGE. Do you have any further evidence to submit, Mr. Gayley?

FRED. I have, Your Honor. *(Rising, he holds a World Almanac in his hand.)* It concerns the postal service, an official agency of the United States government. *(Reading from book.)* The Post Office Department was created July 26, 1776, by the Second Continental Congress, the first postmaster general was Benjamin Franklin. The Post Office Department was discontinued as a part of the president's Cabinet in 1971 and converted to a separate agency which operates its own budget...

MARA. It is indeed gratifying to know about the United States Postal Service, but I hardly think it has any bearing on the present case...

FRED. Begging your pardon, Ms. Mara, it has a great deal of bearing. Your Honor, if I may be allowed to proceed...

JUDGE. By all means.

FRED. I can quote endless details from this volume to verify that the postal service is an efficiently run governmental organization. Moreover, it became an official branch of the federal government just 22 days after the Declaration of Independence was signed. According to its regulations, all positions are governed by civil service procedures. Promotions are based strictly on merit. Furthermore, *postal regulations make it a criminal offense to deliver mail to the wrong party.*

MARA. Your Honor, the state of New York is second to none in its admiration of the United States Postal Service.

FRED *(to the JUDGE)* Will the court accept the U.S. Postal Service as a valid authority for evidence in this case?

MARA. The state of New York will concede that the postal service is an authoritative organization.

FRED. For the record?

MARA. Yes, for the record. Anything to get on with this hearing.

FRED. I wish to introduce three pieces of evidence, Your Honor. Let these be marked "Exhibits A, B and C." *(Hands them to clerk of the court.)* These letters are addressed to "Santa Claus, U.S.A." in childish handwriting. These letters have just now been delivered to Mr. Kringle here in this building by the U.S. Postal Service. I submit, Your Honor, that this is positive proof that a competent federal authority recognizes Mr. Kringle to be the one and only Santa Claus. *(Courtroom reacts mildly. Gavel.)*

MARA. Three envelopes hardly constitute positive proof, Mr. Gayley. I understand the Postal Service receives thousands of such letters every year.

FRED. I have further exhibits, Your Honor, but I hesitate to produce them.

JUDGE. All right, young man. Bring them on. Put them right here on the bench.

MARA *(rich with sarcasm)*. Yes, we'd all like to see them, I'm sure.

FRED. But...Your Honor...

JUDGE. I said put them right here!

FRED. Very well.

(FRED nods toward door. Doors open and many ATTEN-DANTS bring in bags and bags of mail. Courtroom breaks out in pandemonium.)

FRED. Your Honor, every one of these letters is addressed to Santa Claus. *(ATTENDANTS dump bags on Judge's bench.)*
JUDGE *(pounds gavel)*. All right! The United States of America believes this man is Santa Claus. This court will not dispute it... Case dismissed! *(Slow fade on the crowd in pandemonium.)*

SCENE ELEVEN

SCENE: *A suburban street, the following day.*

FRED, DORIS and SUSAN are walking along street. In background is door of a house with the numbers "1225" in gold letters and a "For Sale" sign. They do not immedi-ately notice.

DORIS. This is the best Christmas I have ever had. It was wonderful having dinner with Kris and Doctor Pierce.
SUSAN. All it needs now to make it perfect is snow.
DORIS. I've never had a feeling like this. Fred, for the first time I understand what you mean when you say, "Faith is believing in things..."
ALL THREE *(together)*. "...when common sense tells you not to."
SUSAN *(seeing the house)*. Oh, look! It's my house! It's my house! *(She dashes off into the house.)*
FRED. What does she mean "her house"?

DORIS. I don't know. She has never mentioned anything about a house to me.

FRED. It's a nice-looking house. Probably would be a good real estate investment for somebody.

DORIS. I suppose so.

FRED. Of course, it looks a little big for just two people. It might be a perfect size for three...don't you think? *(DORIS is beginning to get his point. They laugh.)* Doris, you know I've loved you for a long time. And I've loved Susan even longer. Now...don't you think it's time we...

DORIS. Yes, Fred. *(A long kiss.)*

FRED. Maybe we should get this house for Susan.

DORIS. For all of us.

SUSAN *(returning with a cane—very excited)*. Mother!... It's got a swing in the backyard... Just like my dream... Just like my Christmas wish—the one I told Kris about!

DORIS. Susan, Fred and I have something to tell you.

SUSAN. That you're getting married. I know, because that was a part of my Christmas wish too.

FRED *(laughing)*. She's way ahead of us!

SUSAN. And look what I found inside. It was right beside the fireplace. *(She shows Kris' cane. Lights fade as the three of them huddle affectionately together. Snow begins falling.)*

END OF PLAY

Suggestions for Directors:

(1) Have cast members bring in their junk mail throughout rehearsals to fill the bags of "Santa Claus mail" that get poured on the judge's bench in Act Two.

(2) Add music, particularly when Kris is walking with carolers, and with kissing scenes. Carolers during scene changes add a nice holiday touch.

(3) If "Elf Theater" (Act One, Scene Six) is included, it will provide an opportunity for local talented young people to display their skills. Or if that is not possible, this interlude can be a bit of simple choreography or acrobatics, giving young people a chance to entertain.

(4) Elves can be used for changing scenes as their costumes would add to the atmosphere.

(5) Stagehands (other than elves) can be used to carry in the bags of mail in the court scene; also as shoppers walking through the store and pedestrians on the street.

(6) If the production uses carolers during scene changes, these persons may double as an on-stage "audience" during the court scene.

NOTES

NOTES